# Bird Slips, Moon Glows

Linda H.Y. Hegland

ISBN: 978-81-943485-7-3

First Edition: 2019
Rs. 200/-

Cyberwit.net
HIG 45 Kaushambi Kunj, Kalindipuram
Allahabad - 211011 (U.P.) India
http://www.cyberwit.net
Tel: +(91) 9415091004 +(91) (532) 2552257
E-mail: info@cyberwit.net



Printed at Repro India Limited.

Dedicated to my high school counsellor . . . who said that because I was so good with words I should become a secretary.

I never became a secretary, sir.

# Listen

Seek your small, bare rhythm
inside the thrumming cadence
of wind, and water,
birdsong, and quivering fish.
          Listen to the feat of becoming.

How it first whispers
in the shell held to your ear,
then gorges with booming water rush,
or the crack of storm-pitched trees,
          or the shuffle of plunging snow.

Our conversations, then, could be like that of birds
as they scud from branch to branch in the forest.
Call and echo. Co-creation.
Offering quavers and intimate overtures.
          You to me; me to you.

Or like river murmur,
fervent bank-enclosed susurration;
the flowing of words, and silences
in that wet, ecstatic place between shores.
Or like the tone of transmutation in the
          blushing turn of autumn leaves.

Listen to the bruised sighs of those leaves as they fall;
to what the river rumours and what the sky imagines.
Listen, listen, to our own hungry, fierce throb –
          the tremble, the flutter.

But listen to my graceless heart,
in those very places where I am defenseless,
and the owl is enigmatic. Recalls secrets.
Where there is a door that is un-shut,
and a window where the view is luminous.
          Where we bear witness, the otter and I, each to the other.

# Covenant

If I were a leaf trembling and about to fall,
    and you were the ground beneath,
I would waft, pleasingly
    tempting, the wind catching and lofting me,
shuddering me, allowing me to dance
    and tease you.

If you were the ground beneath
    you would wait patiently,
soil pliant and waiting;
    when finally we touched
you would hold me lightly upon yourself,
    hold me as my foliage dress disintegrated,
'til my leaf-bones lay exposed and fragile.

Hold me until even those fragile bits
    became as nothing,
and I became no more a whispering and clattering
    sun worshipper
but a part of you, ground,
    brown and fetid, moist and rotted,
bearer of life and seed.

## When . . . On the Prairie #1

When as a child,
I sit at the foot of the prairie,
crouched in dust and shattered grass,
grasshoppers tangling themselves
in my wind-tattered hair,
I fill my mouth with pebbles and stones.

My tongue moves them round my mouth,
explores the shapes and iron taste.
I feel the smoothness in equal part with the hardness –
the silk with the endurance,
the facility with the clumsiness.

A long meditation
as I sit with the prairie,
sucking on ancient stone and bird-egg pebbles.

# When . . . On the Prairie #2

When as a young woman,
trying desperately to look candid
with wind, always wind on my face,
a hand sheltering my eyes from the sun,
I scuff with my booted toe
bird bones in the dust,
revealed on a day
when the gossamer wind, always wind
stirs the silted ground.

Bird bones thin as glass,
hollow as reeds,
as light in the bluing sky as a mote of dust,
or a drop of rain.
Now mere memory
on a hot, friable day
when grasshoppers jump with a rattle
and hawks keen in the eye-scorching sky,
bones and dust stirred together
by the touch of that gossamer wind.

# When . . . On the Prairie #3

When as an old woman,
I walk the rambling fence line
in the purple mauve pink evening,
with an old dog that promises loyalty
but chases hopefully after gophers and gnarls at magpies
at further and further distances from my side.

I find that there are such things as tumbleweeds
and that they do pledge their love,
just as old Marty said in his old cowboy song.
They blow to my legs and my hips
and whisper don't leave, . . . don't leave.

And I see the wisps of things that came, also, to this fence
leaving scraps of themselves behind.
The hair of red cattle, the wool of black sheep,
the bones of a mouse picked clean
by a muttering owl.

And later, when the lupid moon hangs heavy and
luminous in the umbrae sky,
and the frogs have stilled their trill to a . . . breathlessness;
when the prairie night wind gust-whispers round my ears
and the coyotes begin their banshee songs;

The drive-weary calves move restless,
mourn for their mothers,
Scud their tongues round their lips,
dreaming of mother milk and warm flanks.

I sing to still them, to calm them with a mother-bellow-like run of notes,
taking the call of the yodel-perfect coyotes and turning it to lullaby.
The sounds I sing curl round me and calf alike,
and our loneliness
tucks itself behind the moon.

## Stone, Beloved

Small ancient stone, found,
on dust-choked prairie,
whale-shaped obsidian;
allegories flowing in its veins and channels.

It whispers soundless stories.
Says – listen.

Once waters of a vast river
danced upon my surface.

I held the spawn of fish.

Once I flew high over long grasses
in the talons of a hawk.

Mistaken for bone.

Once I scraped flesh from hides of buffalo,
and hewed the flesh from trees.

Listen.

When first you pick me up from
the prairie floor;
blow the dust from me with lips pursed,
as though to kiss . . .

When first you run your thumb
along my burnished length,
as a lover would another . . .

When first I feel warm again,
held in human hands.
No mere stone . . .

When first I sense your contemplation on
my shape, my form;
the solace you draw from
the stroking of my skin;

I breathe.

I breathe.

# Not That Kind of Daughter

She swirled tea in the pot, jasmine flowers in the brew bloomed like stars in a night sky. The teabags' strings tangled; she remembered she had never been able to do a cat's cradle. A game little girls played, twisting and looping strings around one's fingers. Her mass of string formed knots and lumps, like a pot of over-cooked oatmeal. Soon no one asked her to play cat's cradle. Couldn't skip rope; couldn't pick up jacks. Stones thrown too far in hopscotch, under the bushes and out of sight. Never successful at being a little girl, nor at being a daughter. Not the sort of daughter that her mother wanted. The proud woman who had been her mother. With the kind of looks that adorned garages and barracks. Long legs, bright red lipstick, curves, and cautious eyes. Wolf whistles from men; scornful asides from women. The mother wanted a lot, more. To be a woman of manipulation, haughtiness, calculation. Wanting a daughter with golden curls and baby-doll eyes. And when they emigrated from a country small to a country large. They flew on an airplane – the baby brother, the mother, and the little girl. The father emigrated six months before, would be waiting for them. She remembers nothing but that the brother was ill and cried all the time, all the time. Landing in a big city airport late at night, nowhere to buy food or drink. Not a blind bit of difference the mother said, only small change in her pocket. The mother now crying with the baby brother. The little girl was courageous, she did not cry; she is sure she remembered that she did not cry. Stewardess takes pity and brings stale sandwiches from the plane. They ate small bites, ham and cheese sandwiches, through the early dark hours and into the next day. The next morning, the father was still not there. They waited a long time – and he was still not there. The mother set their suitcases in the middle of the airport terminal. She laid baby brother, finally sleeping, on the floor atop his heavy blue pea jacket, smelling of dried, vomited ham and cheese sandwiches. She sat the little girl, in her red, felt princess coat and matching bonnet on top of one of the suitcases. She scowled at the little girl's soiled, white socks. The mother smoothed bright red lipstick on pale, pale lips. Pulled a comb through disheveled hair, sat down on the other suitcase; tears long dried, eyes and expression hardened. People, people, many people, had to move around them. Porters stopped and maneuvered loaded carts around them. The mother sat with wool coat tucked around knees, silk-stockinged legs placed primly side by side. She smoked a cigarette. When pulled from her lips the little girl could see a red-lipsticked corona around the end. She watched the cigarette grow shorter and shorter. The mother didn't speak to her. The mother was as silent as birds before a storm. She was a good girl, the little girl. She sat still and quiet. The mother ground the cigarette beneath the heel of her shoe. The little girl watched the mother light another cigarette, head high and patrician. And then another and then another. The father arrived hours late, not alone. He brought another man. The mother would not show anger in front of a stranger. The father knew this. This man, the father said, had offered his car to take them home. The man was jovial, pinched the little girl's cheek. It hurt and she didn't smile. Somber-sides, he called her, and lifted the sleeping brother up from the floor. Wrinkled his nose and handed him off to the father, took the suitcases instead. The mother took the little girl's hand, she must have taken her hand, and marched smartly ahead of the father and the friend, leaving a dozen red-stained cigarette butts ground into the glossy linoleum. The little girl stumbled along beside the mother, wishing she could be as haughty, as disdainful, as sure as the mother was that the men would scurry along in her wake, fearing her derision and contempt. But she was not that kind of daughter.

## Stars Like Dandelion Seeds, Scatter and Fall

I once saw a star tumble from the sky;
it sighed and sizzled as it kissed
the earth's thin nimbus,
then consumed itself within its own passion.

I once saw a small bird tumble from the sky;
the breathy hand of a passing breeze caught it
and perched it on a branch.

I once saw a butterfly emerge from its cocoon –
over hours and hours –
its trembling body fragile and tender,
its wings shatter-able like stained glass.
It dried and grew in substance and tenacity;
wings of glass, heart of oak.
It flew away, now shivering with yearning,
fields of colour spread before it.

I once saw, on a sheer rock face –
granite and scree –
a crippled and warped tree.
It grew from a thumb of soil,
drank from the rain in the wind,
adored the sun in its own broken way.
It grew because it didn't know how not to,
its seed an augury of purpose.

I once saw a bee dance, and heard prairie grass sing.

## Watching My Mother Die

My mother lay, moonlight at her feet,
starched, white sheets enshrouding her,
brutal wires and pulsing tubes limining her body like an Old World map.

I focused on just the corner of her mouth,
rolling an imaginary telescope tight
so her mouth (sweet kisses, murmured songs) could not be imputed to her face.

The corner of her mouth then
became like a raindrop on a windowpane,
slowly responding to gravity (grace),
changing shape, becoming and unbecoming,
as it drew close to the force that pulled it to itself.

At one point my mother blew
gently out of her mouth, a final sorrow;
and it was like when one raindrop meets another
on its descent down the glass -
it embraced the breath shape and veered gracefully
in another direction.

My mother sighed, face up,
the corner of her moth flattened and smoothed
like the raindrop when it puddles on the sill
and then runs along the line of the pane -
dissipating to nothingness.

Like my mother, moonlight at her feet.

## Rooted in Surrender

I find the fine, white scar
on my hand;
the result of a frightening question.
It sits in the webbed roots of
bones and veins and the wear of time.
When did my hands turn to oak?
When did my skin turn to paper?
I place my hand on the soil,
also cracked and lined and webbed -
commonality, coincidence,
a universal sigh.

# Ode to a Strawberry

Little hole in you,
juice weeping,
something has experienced
you before

I taste the tear, the tear
Bite

Your tears stain my fingers
my lips

I hold you by your green root,
see your white heart pulse;
you are all-giving

The stain of you indelible

# Bees Drink the Sky Off the Surface of the Water

Murmur, murmur.
I sit with the bees;
it is a meditation
and I feel the hive mind surround me,
hold me,
and expand my body - cellular - spiritual.
Am I healer - like them?
Am I dancer - like them?
Am I artist and builder of universes - like them?

Small, exquisite lives,
bee-murmur, loud quiet
join murmur of blood through
my veins.

I dance with the bees in my heart.

## But you are not like river stones . . .

We are all star stuff
and what is a pebble if not made of stars?
Every pebble a story, a quest;
with a single pebble, the pebble
I choose to pick up and

place in my pocket,
I am carried into the abyssal depths of time,
across the complexity of the universe.
It may speak of the molten purging
of an erupting volcano,

of the lives and deaths of ancient animals,
giant plants,
long ago oceans
and colliding earthen hearts.
It may be small and ordinary,

not even pretty;
but it carries, like me,
stardust at its core -
its single pebble oratory is a story
of all times and all ways of being.

## Heart in Pieces

Is it my fortune or my misfortune that I love too hard?
That I am almost always breakable?
I offer my heart on an open palm that is
lined with my future, or not, as it may be;
appearing at times like a festering aching -
pulsing, pulsing. Contemptible.
At times, other, expansive and moist -
pulsing, pulsing. Animate and mortal.
Could you love me then? Or must I offer more?

And when I sit at the lapping brink of the sea,
toes curled in cinnamon sand,
tearing my space, handful by handful
from fervent crabs, intent on taking it back;
my salt-crusted hair bites at my face.
I am becoming like that wife of Lot.
But I look back. I always look back.
Could you love me then? Or must I soften, waste away?
Until I am, too, a grain of sand? A grain of salt?

I envy those that love less than I;
my envy lies like an emerald at the bottom of my heart,
green and sharp-edged like a blade of grass.
Slicing, slicing,
until I am transparent and fragile.
Could you love me then? Or must I shatter?

Your silly, illogical ways; your suspicious and mutinous soul
hold me at bay. I sacrifice.

I prune my desire – the branches of my heart that reach too far.
I shake the bearded awns of my hunger, the seeds are blown;
my heart is blown.
Could you love me then? Could you love me then?

## Bird Slips, Moon Glows

Bird falls down drifts
of wind,
tossed by storm and chance.

Longs for the succor of dry leaf
and moss, soft,
wings bruised.

In the chilling night,
communion. Slips into
fur of fox, or skin of
wild human. Says . . .

I'll grow my hair long and tangled
again;
let jaw and tongue
sing the song.

Of bird
climbing the last light
of the moon.

# Seeking – Skin to Skin

You and I, child,
we see these
different landscapes.
You see the ants, all in a row,
carrying another, dead from cold.

I see the crow, skittering
from tree to tree -
following, attending, waiting,
watching, abiding.

But your feet are firm on earth,
you don't look up to the sky.
You point out the erosion at
the edges of the alley;
how our path has narrowed
from the year before.

Still,
erosion, growth, or death –
it is all change.

I still see the crow, he sniggers blackly.

Down there, child, where you watch,
the frost
has turned dying leaves
into glittering treasures.

How must these jewels appear
to a crow
on the wing?

These frosted gems and weighted stones
and the prosaic tumble of seasons;
one sighted feather at your feet-
now *that* delights you.

Come near, I'll kiss your cold-reddened cheek,
and blow another to our cawing paramour.

# Prairie Prayer

I will tell you of the prairie,
of how it holds me grounded and tethered,
like a hawk's eye to its prey in the grass.
How the sound of the wind has never left my ears – soughing,
shushing meditation of
wind in the coulees.

I will tell you of the prairie,
early morning magpie clatter, mourning doves
in the cottonwoods,
night-hunting coyote slinking through the
storm belt trees;
home in the dawn, blood stain round his jaw.

Summer afternoons filled with meadowlark trill, hot dusty bite of
wind at my earlobes,
at my cracking lips.
Cornflake crunch of sun-bleached grass crushed with the sweet
smell of sage
beneath my feet.
I see rain, though, three days off.

I will tell you of the prairie,
of blue-skied, deep-cold days where the white is too white and I
am blinded and pained,
where the brittle metallic hardness of plants caught by the freeze
shatter at a touch,
like thin glass.

Of the rising sliver of crescent moon in the blighting
cold of winter,
yearning for the yellow droop of fullness;
and in that bitter raw night – the blousy softness of the feathers of
a small bird
fallen dead from its nocturnal perch, fallen to silence.

Long gone from the prairie, its subtlety, its stillness,
its want of echo,
I still feel the stronghold on my senses.
I yearn still for nothing between me and the far horizon, nothing
between me and the sky,
nothing between me and my wandering thoughts;
emptiness and isolation make me confront myself.

Wind blows my body out of balance,
but I learn to let it hold me,
I learn to let the scouring cleanse me.
The sky is so wide and open I can see the end of myself.

I have become far-seeing, I seek horizons –
yet at my feet the smallest of grasshoppers wanders in the
vastness of her own world,
her focus reduced to a single blade of grass.

The prairie has gifted me with stories
so that I may be a storyteller.

The story of walking out into the prairie with
my old, dying horse.
He and I faced into the wind, lifted our noses;

my long hair and his mane tangled together, intertwined, braided as one.
A sign of his illness, my father said,
horses do not turn into the wind.
He knew where he was going, I said, though not aloud.

The story of walking out on the prairie and stumbling upon the desiccated,
half-eaten carcass of an antelope.
And there in her torn, exposed womb the perfect, tender, curled apostrophe of
an infant antelope.
That deep loss abides in me still – makes me want to be gentle with beings.

I wear the prairie -
the prairie wind and sun have etched lines in my face,
the prairie cold has put a squint in my eye.
It is embedded beneath my skin – my sweat smells of sage and sweet grass.
It is lodged in my heart – I long for the loneliness.

It makes my soul ache to be vast – horizon to horizon.

# Cold Heart

The birds swept low.
Embers died in a long-tired fire.
Both wind and water hardened as the winter night approached.
And the horse came back alone.

# Spring Aches

My forsythia has been reckless yellow
and wild for over two weeks now;
my magnolia held her blooms tight
like a shy girl until asked to dance
by a warm day
and has been bold and frantic ever since.

I walk on ground so moist
from winter melt that it seeps up
through my feet,
into my veins, up into my heart
that beats faster with the pulse
of new spring . . .

and brings a flush to my cheek
that is oddly green and sun-bright;
feathers and leaves sprout from my fingertips
and my eyes grow bluer,
crossed with cantering clouds
like the skies above.

## Seven Horses

Myth has it that you can wish on a ninth horse,
your dreams and wishes coming true;
but on that wintry day,
cloud-scabbed sky, greying snow
there were only seven horses.

White thin bony
old beyond old,
hooves slipping on rime-slicked rocks,
sparks flying up into
obsidian frigid air.

(The hoofs of Jehovah's horses are counted as flints – Isa. 5:28)

My sons called them Ghost Horses
as they stared gape-mouthed
at the horse shapes morphing and
transmuting, each with the other,
in the blindness and shuffle-hush
of the fresh snow
falling on frozen ground.

I will not speak of portent or omen,
of wishes or dreams;
but I will speak of ancient
horses that flew
sparks from their hooves
and blew their equine breath
with pink-rimmed snorts into the winter cold;

and had only the power of seven.

# Naming Bird

Grassland fingers
reach for the river,
searching for the names of things;
naming empathy and that spotted
frog on the river's shore.

Sage leans into
the rising hills
where the deer come
only for the salt,
not remembering their name.

Now! Name the being with wings
that looks at you
with a question
in its eye.
You have only to name to know.

Bird.

# Unknowing

I did not know you loved so much
the sharp-sharded broken jars
lining the windowsills, dust-smoked;
the ones that once held wildflowers
that lasted only a day,
or stones from the lake shore – just the rust ones, or blue,
or the dropped feathers of fled birds, iridescent,
as though the sun still shone in their shafts.

I did not know you loved so much
sunflowers at the moment
they are closest to death;
bent parched heads
touching the earth, kissing the dust,
anointing it with fecund seed -
the unction, the covenant.

I did not know you loved so much
the old mare that died
in the storm of a winter so cruel
birds fells frozen from the air,
their wings outstretched,
their haloes bent from the fall.

I did not know you loved so much
that strange muted place
by the tumulus in the forest;
where the water speaks your name

and the trees innately know
the time of your birth.

I did not know you loved so much
the stars of a winter sky – brightest, sharpest.
Or the hares on the snowdrifts
when they stare,
moonstruck,
singing their silent chorus
with faces upturned.

I did not know you loved so much.
How could I have not known
you loved
so much.

## Crows at Twilight

Old crow,
solitary in the light of day;
abrupt nod to others
as two or three together
root through the same
found treasure in the middle of the road.

Twilight descends;
sky darkens
with hordes of crows, murders of crows,
veritable massacres of crows,
reeling, cawing, black on black, soot on twilight sky.

Roosting in trees,
fashioning for trees
black-feathered foliage.
Roosting in trees, gathering omens and fates
to distribute like storks
to expectant breath-held families.

Black eyes glitter like obsidian,
black pools with moon reflected.
The pendulum weight of meeting with crows,
ruing, exalting,
the turn in the road to be taken - or not,
the conversations to be had.

# Drawing from Life – a Body of Time

*(Renderings by an Art Student)*

That body up there,
still and taut on the podium,
exposed, vulnerable,
yet silently crying out with
the story it has to tell,
the history it has to relate,
the journey it has to map.

I look to the shapes,
and the lines,
and the scars;
the tools in my fingers
are my narrator:
sultry charcoal and conte, stark pen and ink,
soft and secretive pastels.

Pen and ink for a young man's body
lean, spare and angular;
my renderings quick, gestural and spontaneous;
he as subject, me as artist – our expectations of each other
are exacting and unforgiving.
Lines are drawn that demand perfection,
allowing no room for error.

Another day, another story, a woman thick with child -
charcoal;
the lines smeared smudges,
the shape of her body simply suggested,

the kindness of a softer touch, a softer medium,
my hot fingers obliterate the lines,
disappear the shapes into each other.

Another day, another history;
a woman aged, her body worn,
I wish to gift her with light -
render her in soft pastels
and forgive the sagging lines and scars
of a well-lived-in body that is so, so tired.

I hang the drawings with thumbtacks on the wall -
drawings from life, a body of time.

## Suzanne

When Leonard Cohen sang of Suzanne
and of being taken to the water,
we bare-footed, Rapunzel-haired,
gypsy-dancing girls
all thought he sang of *us.*
We each believed we *were* the Suzanne
that Lennie sang of in his
whiskied, whispering voice.

We had lovers who were poets
and, by being so, were doomed
to mutter lifeless words in smoky cafes.
We sang plaintive songs
on out-of-tune guitars and
wore far too many scarves
about our necks and hair
and waists.

We made love in dirty sheets
until the sun climbed to noon,
and swam naked in chilly lakes
until the moon rose.
We wrote our own heart-jagged poetry
steeped in angst and bruised emotions,
and danced in the rain
despite the skeeters and the mud.

But once I received a note
from a stranger in a bar

who saw me drunk and giddy,
with my hair across my damp cheeks
and clinging to my neck, my eyes too bright.
The note said “you lift my heart, you lovely girl,
wishing you cascades of lilies”.
No doubt, I am the real Suzanne.

## Time at Bay

At the edge of the ocean,
meditating on time, playing
word games with myself on the
contrapuntal music of time –
infinity, lifetime, moon counting,
lastingness, season, eternity,
moment, tempo, day, night,
past, future . . . tide.

Children blur by me,
bolting from wave to shore,
from shore to stone;
tail-gating, bent to a destination.
I ricochet off the current they cause
like a mote of dust in the wind;
my time is slow to their fast,
another dimension – unseen.

Old man lumbers past in a suit
soaked with salt water,
he carries an old briefcase
of rusty cracked leather.
His salt-rimed face carries the musings and
ruinations in his mind, his lips
muttering arguments with himself;
he takes the time to think fully on them.

# Publications

*Listen* previously published in Sky Island Journal, Issue 4, Spring 2018

*Stone, Beloved* previously published in Sky Island Journal, Issue 3, Winter 2018

*Covenant* is a winner of Cecilia Lamont Poetry Competition, Fall 2017

*When . . . On the Prairie #1* previously published in Sky Island Journal, Issue 1, Summer 2017

*When . . . On the Prairie #2* previously published in Sky Island Journal, Issue 1, Summer 2017

*When . . . On the Prairie #3* previously published in Sky Island Journal, Issue 1, Summer 2017

*Not That Kind of Daughter* previously published in Unbroken Journal, May/june 2015, nominated for Pushcart Prize

*Stars like Dandelion Seeds, Scatter and Fall* previously published in The American Aesthetic, Volume 3, Spring 2015

*Watching My Mother Die* previously published in Hermeneutic Chaos, Issue 1, May 2014 and also in ArtAscent, February 2015, awarded Distinquished Writer.

*Rooted in Surrender* previously published in Bricolage Magazine of Independent Arts & Culture, Issue 3, 2013.

*Ode to a Strawberry* previously published in Bricolage Magazine of Independent Arts & Culture, Issue 3, 2013

*Bees Drink the Sky Off the Surface of the Water* previously published in Bricolage Magazine of Independent Arts & Culture, Issue 3, 2013

*But you are not like river stones . . .* previously published in Bricolage Magazine of Independent Arts & Culture, Issue 3, 2013

An excerpt from *Prairie Prayer* was published in the Prairie Journal of Canadian Literature, Issue #60, 2013.

www.ingramcontent.com/pod-product-compliance
Lightning Source LLC
Chambersburg PA
CBHW022203160726
48282CB00024B/316
* 9 7 8 8 1 9 4 3 4 8 5 7 3 *